Time Management

Breezing Through Your Day Easily

By

Fhilcar Faunillan

Les Ilagan

Cocktails and More

The information provided herein is stated to be truthful and consistent, in that any liability, in terms of inattention or otherwise, by any usage or abuse of any policies, processes, or directions contained within is the solitary and utter responsibility of the recipient reader. Under no circumstances will any legal responsibility or blame be held against the publisher for any reparation, damages, or monetary loss due to the information herein, either directly or indirectly.

Respective authors own all copyrights not held by the publisher.

The information herein is offered for informational purposes solely, and is universal as so. The presentation of the information is without contract or any type of guarantee assurance.

The trademarks that are used are without any consent, and the publication of the trademark is without permission or backing by the trademark owner. All trademarks and brands within this book are for clarifying purposes only and are the owned by the owners themselves, not affiliated with this document.

Table of Contents

INTRODUCTION

I want to thank you and congratulate you for downloading the book, *"Time Management: Breezing Through Your Day Easily"*.

We can have so many limitations in this lifetime but nothing limits us more than time. Time is the only resource in the world by which all people become equal. You, me and every person in the world regardless of age, gender and nationality receives 24 hours each day. But the question is how can some people do more with their 24 hours than I do or than you do? The answer lies in proper time management. Time management can spell the difference between failure and success in a person's life so if you want to be successful then this is the right book for you.

Discover what time management is all about and understand its value in Chapter

1. This book will let you look at time management as a skill which will require a set of skills and some habits in it. In Chapter 2, you will be learning your first skill which is to set and name your goals. Another thing you must learn is how to prioritize your tasks which will be discussed in Chapter 3. You will see how best to plot your day as I share to you some tips in blocking your time in Chapter 4. Chapter 5 will be all about creating a productive workplace for you because believe it or not, what you can achieve is also a function of your direct environment. Then we will be tackling a very talked-about issue in time management – procrastination. Why do we procrastinate? How can we stop ourselves from procrastinating? Discover the answers to these questions in chapter 6.

With the five skills I have presented above, this book will also share to you some habits you can adopt and at the same time open your eyes to dangerous habits you should avoid. Chapter 7 will teach your practices to hone your focus and concentration when there is an important task at hand. To complement this, you will also receive some important tips on how to make the most out of your time through some time-efficient habits in Chapter 8. Lastly, let this book open your eyes to the most common time-wasting habits that you might have so that you can try and avoid them in the future. This will be tackled in the last chapter.

Thanks again for downloading this book, I hope you enjoy it and may the proven steps and strategies in this book help you in increasing productivity and more happiness!

Chapter 1
Understanding The Value of Time Management

Saying that time is the most precious and most valuable gift anyone can offer someone holds a lot of truth. I am sure you have heard of this before but some of you might wonder how time could be better than, say, money or material possessions. What you fail to see is that time is something that when given, cannot be earned or taken back. The day that your significant other spent to be with you is a day lost in his life to pursue his other dreams. The times your mother spent guiding you as you grow is the same amount of time that she had deprived herself of thinking about her own growth.

Based on what I have just said, you can easily see that time is a resource that is different from other resources we are familiar with. For one, time is the only resource where every person, no matter their gender, social status, or nationality, is endowed with the same amount of. Each of us has only 24 hours, 1440 minutes or 86,400 in a day and nobody gets more or less. Another reason is that time is a resource that cannot be accumulated. When we do not feel like doing an important task today, we cannot reserve our precious minutes for later use once we are ready to face what we must. In simpler terms, we cannot turn on or off time just when we like it, whether we are productive or not in a given time, it becomes a time past that cannot be brought back.

Time just slips from our fingers, whether we like it or not. I am sure that many of you have experienced having so many things to accomplish and when the deadline has arrived, we wonder where has all the time go because we have achieved nothing. Things like this happen not just in small projects like reaction papers in school but also to career-changing proposals at work. The sad thing here is that you can't take back the time you have wasted not doing what you must have done and it is this very nature of time that makes it even more important and this is where time management comes into play.

Cocktails and More

The fact that you are reading this book can mean that you have some idea of what time management is all about. I mean topics and articles of time management is everywhere from magazines to television shows so how can you not? But for knowledge's sake, time management is basically the process of planning specific tasks and allocating time for them such that you can achieve the results you desire.

So let me ask, how can time management help you? One important lesson we know in our hearts but may not have acknowledged out loud is that understanding is the basic prerequisite of motivation. We cannot be motivated to do something unless we know what we are doing it for. That is why in this chapter, we will be drawing the line that connects time management with success. Before we go on to the steps you must take for mastering time management, here are some of its benefits for a huge motivation-booster.

1.   *You can be more productive.*

When we fail to set specific plans for the day and fail to allocate time for each task, we often end up forgetting the most important task or maybe use so much time for an insignificant project. At the end of the day, we feel disappointed with ourselves upon the realization that we have achieved nothing. With time management though and strict compliance to it, we are sure to achieve something with our time.

2.   You become more efficient.

Not only do you become more productive with proper time management but you also become more efficient. When you plan your tasks, you don't end up buying your groceries first before cleaning the kitchen such that you won't miss an item on your shopping list and have to visit the store twice in a day.

3.   Time management brings less guilt and stress

When you are used to postponing important tasks despite looming deadlines, you probably know how stressful the event can be. You have to stay up overnight to make up for the lost time and you sometimes even doubt yourself if you can make it on time. Stress isn't even the only emotion bothering you when these situations arise. There is also that guilt and maybe some self-loathing of not having used your time more productively and efficiently. Thankfully, with time management, you can easily get rid of these problems in the future.

4.   You create more opportunities for yourself.

We want so many things in life such as learning a new language, visiting a new place or having more time with our loved ones. And yet, for us who have busy schedules or think that we are "busy" (even when we actually are not), it is quite impossible to achieve these things. But the truth, we are actually the very people who create opportunities for ourselves. You are the one who open yourself for your opportunity. So when we know what we want, we plan what we want, we can make the opportunity come in our doorstep. Can you believe that that opportunity can be achieved with time management?

5.   *You can plot time for yourself, too!*

Busy is such a subjective word. A company CEO will consider himself busy, a regular employee will consider himself busy and a student will consider himself busy as well. In our very busy schedules doing what we think needs to be done or just maybe deciding whether we have to start the task right now or postpone it for later, we sometimes forget that we need sometime for ourselves too. We usually overwork, oversleep and over think that we fail to realize that we need to allocate sometime for ourselves. We think that we are too busy but then when we plan our time well, we will realize that we actually have small but valuable chunks of time doing nothing at all. When we plan our week well, a free Saturday can be a reward ourselves. Finally, we can do what we want without any guilt.

With the numerous benefits that time management can bring you, I am sure that you are now very eager to learn about proven strategies and tips you can use. Now is the time for you to start your journey towards effective use of your time for you to be able to breeze through your day easily.

Chapter 2
Naming and Setting Goals

No time management book would be complete without a discussion on goal-setting. What makes goal setting so important? The biggest reason is that goal setting provides us with direction. In our hearts, we all want to achieve something or go somewhere. Sometimes we become too lazy to introspect and just leave our goals as that: achieve something or go somewhere. But aren't those goals very vague? What do you want to achieve? Where do you want to go? By knowing the specifics of our goal, we can see the connection of what we are doing right now and how it can help us achieve what we want or bring us to where we want to be. In short, goals help you take control of your life.

Your goals can also help you achieve focus in order to limit your detours. If you live each day like a zombie, just going anywhere and travelling any road, you are very likely to end up somewhere you don't want to be. However, when you take note of your goals, you will know whether a certain task will lead you to where you want to be. Thus, you perform less wrong moves and waste little of your precious time.

Another reason is that that knowing your goals can keep your motivations high. You don't just do something for nothing but you exercise every single day because it is your goal to achieve a normal Body Mass Index, you work overtime to achieve a six-digit savings figure and you finish your assignments fast so that you can have the weekend for free. Again, understanding what you want and knowing that what you are doing right now can help you achieve it, just increases your drive to finish it all the more.

We all have hopes, dreams and goals that we want to achieve in our lifetime. Some of our goals are too big that we shy away from doing anything because we have convinced ourselves that we will never be able to achieve them. Sometimes though, our goals are too small that it doesn't challenge us enough for us to really do it. What we don't know is that our ability to achieve our goals is primarily a function of how we set them.

In simpler terms, the more clearly your goals are set, the more likely you are to achieve them. That is why in this chapter

I will be sharing you some important guidelines in goal setting.

1.   Write 'em down!

Do you know that studies suggest that the people who write their clearly defined goals down are the ones who have more money, power, influence and prestige? In short, goal-setters who jot their goals down are more successful. This is because listing your goals is just like preparing a shopping list. It ensures you don't miss a necessary step, action or task that will lead you to what you want. So go and take a piece of paper or your seldom-used planner perhaps and prepare it to start jotting your goals as we go over equally important guidelines below.

2.   Put a name to your goals.

Just to reiterate, you shouldn't just say you want to achieve something or go somewhere. You have to know what you want to achieve and what you want to go. Put a name to your goal. For instance, if you want to exercise as I know you really want to, don't just write "exercise" on your list. Instead, write down the specific exercise you want to accomplish. Do you want aerobic exercises or resistance exercises?

3.   Create measurable goals.

How do you know you have achieved your goal already? You can easily know this when you attach numbers to your goals. For instance, you can say that you have completed your daily exercise when you have finished thirty minutes of aerobic activity or completed five repetitions of a set of exercises. Another reason figures or a certain criteria is important in goal-setting is for you to be able to track your progress towards your goals. If you want a hundred thousand bucks on your bank account, you will know that the thousand dollars you can put there will make you closer to your goal by one percent. Don't you worry if I'm already talking numbers here; these are pretty simple calculations that I am sure you can do too.

4. Dream big and dream possible.

Never think that you have to limit your goals here. You can dream all you want but you also have to make sure that they are within the means of what's humanly and physically possible. In other words, your goals should be attainable. The problem with most of us is that we often shy away from big goals because we think that we cannot do them even if we haven't tried yet. We are very afraid of the disappointment that comes with failing that we never even attempt to pursue it. But the truth is, when we point out big goals and dreams that we really want to achieve, we tend to find ways that will help us get there. Let us not limit our dreams to accommodate our current set attitude, knowledge and skills. Instead, let us change our attitude, expand our knowledge and hone our skills to take on bigger challenges.

5. Break down big goals to manageable tasks.

Yes, I have encouraged you to never limit your goals no matter how big they are but these big goals and dreams might still be overwhelming for you. The trick here is to divide your goals into smaller chunks that you can take on one step at time. Let's just say that these steps are little goals that you have to accomplish to be able to achieve your big goals. For example, you dream of building your own business before you reach the age of 40. To do this, you have to first point out what business do you want to get into, create a plan on where you will get your capital for the business, save a certain amount of money for your capital perhaps, enroll in a business management class, and maybe a lot more. Now your dream doesn't look that impossible anymore knowing that you just have to accomplish one step at a time to eventually get there.

6.   Your goals should be realistic, too!

As I have said earlier, you can dream big as long as it is humanly possible. Realistic goals are sort of similar to the attainable goals in number 4 that has to be possible. In realistic goals however, you not just need the means of achieving goal but you also need the motivation to get there. Again, you don't have to shrink your goals especially when it just other people who thinks that it is unrealistic because trust me, big dreams can become reality when you have the drive to make it one.

7. Set a time frame for each of your goals.

The fact that you have your goal written on your to-do list means that you really have the intention of finishing it. However, just writing specific and measurable goals which are also attainable and realistic are not enough. Your goal should be time-bound to. This means that you have to create a deadline for yourself in finishing your goal and avoid setting a vague point in time that it too far in the future. Setting deadlines for the completion of your goals can create an atmosphere of urgency and efficiency to0 help you fulfill your tasks faster.

In time management, goal setting is definitely a goal you need to master. Now, think about the questions I have raised earlier. What do you want to achieve in this life? Where do you want to go? What places do you dream of visiting? Where do you see yourself ten years from now?

Twenty years from now? Thirty years from now? Write your goals and dream down following the guidelines I have presented and by doing so, you can so easily manage not just your time but your resources as well to get you where you want to be.

Chapter 3

Prioritizing Your Tasks

If you are like me who wants to achieve so many things in my lifetime, you probably have such a long list that you don't even know where to start. The biggest problems we are going to face here are the limitations. We can have limitations on what's socially acceptable to do, we can have limitations in terms of financial resources and of course we also face time limitations. We just have a very limited time on earth and most of it may have probably been gone to waste already. Now that you have been awakened to the multitude of dreams and goals that you want to accomplish, it is time for us to start making our precious hours and minutes useful. But then the question still remains, which task or set of tasks must I do first?

A very important issue you have to face in time management is prioritizing tasks. We have to acknowledge the facts that first, we cannot do everything all at once and second, that we are faced by time constraints and limitations. How do we achieve everything we want to do all in 24 hours and still get some decent sleep? The implication here is that we have to learn which tasks needs to be stricken out from our list first and which tasks can wait until later. For us to be very productive with our time striking as much important tasks from our to-do list we have to work not just efficiently but work effectively as well. We can do that through the proper prioritization of our tasks and here are the steps you can follow to do just that.

1.   Identify your top goals.

You must have hundreds of goals or dreams that you have written in the previous chapter. The next step you are going to take is to identify which among these goals will provide you with the most fulfillment and satisfaction once achieved. In this step we will be applying the Pareto's principle or what we commonly hear as the 20-80 rule. In this rule, you simply had to identify the top 20 percent of your goals which can provide you with 80 percent results. For instance, if you have 50 goals and dreams on your list, pick out the top 10 which will give the satisfaction and the fulfillment that you seek for in this life. For instance, these goals and dreams might be to be able to build your own house, to save funds for your children's college education and to take the family to an out of the country vacation. These are just few big dreams but these dreams may be already give you the most satisfaction.

2.   Create your master list of day-to-day tasks.

Your to-do list or your day-to-day tasks should not consist of the goals or dreams you have written above. Instead this should consist of concrete action plans and steps that will lead you to the fulfillment of your goal. Remember what I said about breaking your goals into manageable pieces? Well it should be manageable enough for you to take baby (or toddler) steps every day. Simply stated, your tasks should be in line with your goals and dreams.

Aside from your concrete action steps, write down anything and everything you need to accomplish for the day. Not only should you put the critical tasks such as turning in a paper but you should also not forget to put even the most mundane task, such as checking your email, in your list. Your routine duties are also tasks that you need to accomplish in a day so make sure you have accounted for it.

3.   Screen out your list.

Most of the time, we are actually the ones who deliberately put ourselves in the most difficult situations. For instance, we take on tasks that aren't really ours to do or we start doing something without even knowing how it can benefit us. So we put ourselves in this crazy-busy situation where we end up forgetting the tasks of more importance that we should be doing instead. That is why it is still important for you to screen out the items on your to-do list based on their importance and urgency in order for you to find out what activities should take your time.

√   Important and Urgent Tasks. If the task at hand is important and at the same time urgent such as a work deadline or a major emergency, then that is something **you have to do now**.

√   Important but Not Urgent. These are the things that **you should plan to do**. Since it is not yet urgent, what you have to do instead is plan its implementation so that when it requires to be done, you can execute your plan smoothly and efficiently.

√   Not Important but Urgent. If these are tasks of grave urgency but are considered unimportant to you, then these are very likely to be just some request of others to you or are merely irrelevant distractions. Do not let these things waste your time and instead learn to say no in a nice manner since these tasks are the things that **you must reject.**

√   Not Important and Not Urgent. What are these tasks doing on your list anyway?

Are these just some useless routines or time-consuming comfort activities? Remember that your time is valuable so **you should stop doing** these things altogether. If you want to learn how to avoid these kinds of things, Chapter 9 will help you how to avoid these time-wasting habits.

Since you will be delegating the third set of tasks that are urgent yet not important and you have probably deleted the fourth set of tasks which are neither important nor urgent, then what is left with you is most likely a visibly shortened list. Isn't that discovery such a relief?

1.   Assign priority levels for each task.

√ With your tasks shorten and shrunk to a minimum, assigning   priority levels for each task will be a breeze. A very common method to do this is to assign letters for each task according to three priority levels.

√ A Tasks – A tasks are the one you must do because they are critical items. They belong to the first category of tasks above which are important and at the same time urgent. Examples of these tasks include deadlines, management directives and opportunities for success or advancement.

√ B Tasks – B tasks are tasks of middle value and are things that you should do but not necessarily now. They technically are important tasks but they are not yet urgent. B Tasks includes those that may contribute to your improved performance but with no critical deadlines.

√ C Tasks – The last category are the C tasks. These types of tasks are those that you should do when the situation permits. These are still important tasks as they could benefit you but you have to leave it for later when the A and B tasks have been fulfilled.

From the steps I have presented, I believe you already know which of the tasks on your to do list needs your desperate attention. It is essential to note that priorities are a matter of perspective. You and not anyone else can best judge what you have to do and you are the best evaluator which among your tasks deserves the highest priority. To be successful in time management, you have to be able to maximize your time and you can do so by focusing on what is important.

Chapter 4
Scheduling Your Day

Now that you know which among the tasks you think you need to do are truly of importance and requires your attention, it's time to begin scheduling your day. In this chapter, I will be teaching you another important skill that you should acquire: "time-blocking." Time-blocking is the skill of dividing your time into small increments (e.g. 15-minute or 30-minute increments) and intelligently placing or arranging your tasks in the time slots to ensure maximum efficiency. Research suggests that time blocking is a very effective time management tool with the most success rates across different areas of your life. Does time-blocking sounds too-OCD for you? Don't you be repulsed by the idea as time-blocking will be a big step for you to take control of your life.

Before we go on to the specifics of time blocking, let me tell you that this skill can be tricky since it requires a lot of adjustment especially for beginners. With consistent and diligent practice though, I am positive that you can do it as we all get better with practice. Now let us start scheduling your day by following these easy steps.

1.   Know your prime time.

Your prime time is your most productive time in a day. I have discovered my prime time when I was in college. I found out that I can read faster from 5:00 to 7:00 o'clock in the morning and I can retain more of what I have read. So I brought that discovery with me even when I am now working as a writer and as a motivational speaker wherein I sleep early so that I can wake up early and find fresh ideas as the sun is rising. By studying and thinking about how you use your time today, you can discover your productivity trends and know your prime time. You can then use this self-knowledge to your advantage by scheduling important activities that requires creativity, concentration and thought during this time.

2. Divide your day to small increments

Now, what you are going to do is to divide your day to small increments. I prefer 15-minute than 30-minute increments because it can be enough to tell you that you can already be productive in such a short amount of time. In addition, dividing your time into small blocks help minimize the time you might waste. When you accidentally skip a task on schedule, it is better to miss a 15-minute task than a 30-minute one.

To divide your day, you are going to need your calendar or planner modified with grids for the 15-minute periods. I really prefer written calendars than the digital ones on our smart phones or tablets because writing them down can make me remember them even when I don't look at my planner throughout the day. Just pick the planner that suits you. In your planner, you have to clearly put a division between your personal time and your work time. Since both these aspects are essential for us to live a healthy and happy life, it has to have balance even from the start. Perhaps you can block your work time as only the weekdays during the office hours and leave everything else to personal time.

3.   Put in your personal activities first

You heard me right; you have to put your personal activities in the planner first. This is because what we do with our personal time is of grave importance to our well-being not be overtaken by secondary obligations. If we do not schedule our personal activities first, we end up sacrificing our precious personal time for work. Trust me, this is what usually happens and I know you are aware of that. You can start by putting your routine activities in your planner such as dinner with the family, a weekly date or the household chores that you must personally attend to. Next input your personal activities which are not routine but make sure that these tasks still supports your priorities.

4. Enter your work activities in the equation

Like the personal activities, you have to schedule first those that work priorities that are routine. For instance, place your weekly or daily meetings and other appointments. Allot time for each activity that you have to accomplish at work, especially those tasks with looming deadlines. You shouldn't forget to factor in the mundane activities at work that you still have to do. That would probably be answering call or checking your email. Make sure that these work activities do not overlap with your personal time.

5. Allot sometime for planning and evaluation

Whether it is business, in war or even in our weekend get together with our family, planning takes an important role. Proper planning ensures that we forget no significant detail and that the execution will go smoothly. As the old adage goes, for every minute we take to plan, we save ten times the execution. In time management, planning is a necessity so we have to take a chunk of time in our calendar and allot it just for planning. Perhaps you can plan for the upcoming week just as the current week ends. This can be on a Friday or Saturday afternoon. Together with planning, you can also evaluate your performance on the previous week on whether you have been productive enough and whether you have met all the tasks and activities you have set for yourself.

6.   Account for flex time

You probably will agree with me that we can never work straight on hours nonstop. Even when we sit in front of our computer for hours, our eyes eventually look far off the distance staring blankly at nothing in particular. Although this is helpful for our eyes to rest, activities like this can throw us off our schedule. That is why it is necessary to account for flex time. These segments of time on your schedule can minimize the fallout due to unplanned problems and interruptions. If you know that there is free time ahead, it would be easier for you to stick to your schedule. You can have a 30-minute flex time for your two hours of time-blocked activity. If you think that this is too much for the tasks you have in hand, you have the freedom to decrease it to 15 minutes. Just an important note, you have to schedule your flex time after critical activities because if it's the other way around, you might get distracted or fail to get started when you will start the critical activity.

Do these steps sound too much? Again, these will require your commitment and diligence but after weeks of practice, you can do this in a breeze. By following your schedules as plotted, I am sure you will find yourself more productive and even more closer to your dreams and goals as each week passes.

Chapter 5
Creating a Productive Workplace

I have this crazy ritual that when I open my book to study and read the first sentence, I stop and put the book down because some things look wrong in my peripheral vision. The papers to my right are not parallel to the table, the pencils and pens are not in its proper position and my slippers on the ground are not placed side-by-side. When I have caught myself doing this in several occasions, I worried that I have obsessive-compulsive disorder but turns out I don't when I read the diagnostic criteria for self-diagnosis. But then I read about procrastination and I discovered that those things I did subconsciously to put of something I do not want to do. I probably am not just in the mood of studying during that time that is why I try my best to put it off even just for minutes. In short, my rituals were just excuses.

There are many other occasions wherein our productivity is decreased by the kind of workplace we have. How many minutes on average do you spend finding your eye glasses or your pen only to find out that it just there in your head? Or how many minutes do you spend in a day looking for one certain paper in the middle of the piles of papers on your desk? Then when you get tired of looking, you have to check with Joana if she really did give you the paper or if it was Charles who received it instead. If you spend 30 minutes on average looking for things because you have a poor workspace, then you waste about 3.5 hours in a week and 14 hours in a month. Imagine what you can do in those 14 hours!

Setting up a productive workspace is necessary as it helps us become more efficient and productive. When we clear are desks and put order in our workplace, we minimize the time doing insignificant activities such as looking for staplers or scanning our news feed even when our primary intention was to see a message when out phone vibrated. Since your workspace can definitely spell the difference between successful time management and no productivity, I have some tips to help you.

1. Tune Out Interruptions

I don't know if you have observed this but we humans are easily distracted. When our bedroom door opens, we turn our head towards it – automatically – even when we know that the only person who will get in is our husband or our wife. When we hear the sound of our email notification, we automatically think about the possible sender of the email and what it must contain and when we get too curious, we end up opening the email, scanning our news feed, reading blogs, see pictures on Instagram and so much more. This sensitivity to distractions or changes in our environment is already hard-wired in the brain so the best we can do is controlling or environment and tuning out interruptions.

What causes delay or disturbance to you when you are working? If you have the answers to the question, make sure you put these things away when you are working. For instance, you can put a "Do Not Disturb" sign on your home office door once you start working and ask your family to abide that rule unless there is a grave emergency. You can turn down the volume of your smart phone and put it out of your reach so that it will not distract you. You can also clear your desktop from icons and make sure what in there are just those that you really need to do. By tuning out these interruptions, you can ensure that you can work smoothly and undisturbed.

2.   Clearing up your desk

If your excuse of not clearing up your desk is because you have survived all these time in chaos, then imagine your productivity levels without your chaotic desk. It will probably shoot up! For most of us, our desk is our primary workspace which means that this is where we must be productive. It also translates that when our desk is such a mess, we also decrease our productivity levels. This is because a topsy-turvy desk gives the illusion of having so many things to do and that can increase the chances of procrastination. So be very brutal in clearing of the clutter. Move your photos elsewhere or hang them by the wall. Store office tools, especially the rarely used ones, on desk drawers. Put the items that you haven't even looked at away and into the filing cabinet. At first you may still have a lot of things on your desk but if you continue this practice, what will be left on it are just the really essential ones.

3.   Use organizational tools

One reason why we spend so much time looking for something is not assigning an area for these items. Taking advantage of organizational tools that can add order to our workplace can help us work smoothly. There are many organizational tools available in bookstores that you can set up in your office. You can use desk organizers for the office tools and supplies, inboxes and outboxes to reduce questions and chitchats from coworkers, colored file folders for your different tasks at work and a lot more.

4.   Keep the clutter from coming back

I am sure you have tried cleaning your office or desk before and try to look at it now if you have maintained the cleanliness. If you have not, then you have probably prevented the clutter from coming back. The technique to avoid these clutters in staying at your desk and cause chaos is to handle them once. Yes, handle them just once. Dump it if you don't need it, delegate it if you know that it is somebody else's job or that somebody can do it better, detour it to a particular folder on your desk if you cannot attend to it at the moment and do it if the paper that is vying for your attention is urgent or is simple enough to not take too much of your time.

You may not be able to control your time but the good thing here is that you can control your environment. When you create and maintain your productive workspace, you can definitely see an increase in your performance in no time.

Chapter 6

Combatting Procrastination Problems

Admit it, for once or many times in your life, you have been a victim or procrastination. There might be some project that was given ages ago that you kept at the back of your mind and when the deadline is very closely approaching, you have produced mediocre results instead. What's sad is that you know you could've done better if only you had time. What's even sadder is that you already had the time; you just didn't use it well.

Procrastination can be dangerous and stressful for us but why do we still procrastinate? Before we tackle why we procrastinate, we need to know our enemy first. We procrastinate for various reasons and here are the most common excuses we use so often we no longer believe in them.

1.   We have too much time.

Our teachers and our bosses give us plenty of time for a certain project for a reason: it needs time to be completed. But the tendency is that when we are given a task, we don't start with it right away because we think that we still have too much time. Fast-forward to the day right before the deadline and we notice our precious hours seem to fly by so fast. This short-sighted logic is one of the most common reasons why we procrastinate.

2.   We put off unpleasant tasks.

When there is a project or task you do not want to do, it is so easy putting it off for later. Humans as we are, we have the tendency to steer away from uncomfortable situations such as a difficult project or a confrontation with someone. We let our emotions take over and convince ourselves to just do it later.

3.   We are afraid of failing.

These are true words whether you like to hear it or not: one reason why we procrastinate is that we do not trust ourselves of being able to succeed in a project. We might be unsure of our abilities if we can actually do it so we postpone starting the task on the eleventh hour. Because honestly, it is much easier to blame time constraints for our failure rather than our own inability, right?

4. We want to wait for the right time.

We often hear this excuse for not doing something. We usually wait for the right time to come and this right time usually consists of us having the motivation to start the project or being in the right mind frame. But the question we fail to ask ourselves is that if this is not the right time, then when is it? We don't do something because we lack the motivation to do it when in fact we can just easily find the motivation when we start doing it.

5. We work under pressure.

This is such an overused excuse for not postponing a task. But do you know that studies show that time constraints more often than not translate to poor performance? When we work under pressure, we no longer have time to let our creative juices flow, we have poor problem-solving skills and we lack the time to review our work resulting to mediocre results.

It is truly amazing how the human mind can justify procrastination. We provide a lot of reasons and excuses for not doing something even when we know that procrastinating can result to dire consequences. Procrastinating can cost not only money, time and the quality of our work but our mental and physical well-being as well. Since procrastination is a very important issue that we have to overcome, I have provided tips for you to avoid it.

1. Practice concrete planning strategies.

The reason why we think that we have so much time or that a task is difficult is because we think of the project in abstract ways. We don't think about how long a step will actually take or how easy it is if we break a certain task down. This is why a great way to battle procrastination problems is to think of a task in the most concrete way possible. The images you create in your head should be realistic and close to the future. Think of the task in the context of the day as if it is really happening at the moment. Think of what you have to do to complete the task and how doing these things will make you feel. Adding some figures to the picture will also help such us factoring in how long will each step take for a more concrete picture of what lies ahead for you.

2.   Don't give in to feeling good.

If you are uncomfortable of doing something or if you are afraid of failing, then the more reason for you to start doing what you must right away. If a task makes you uncomfortable, think of how you can get away from the uncomfortable feeling the earlier you finish it. If you are afraid of failing, think of the chances for you to do better once you finish your first try. These emotions don't only get to us before we even start a project. Sometimes, they come to us while we are already doing the task. For instance, we feel bored or frustrated while doing a paper. You should know that it is alright to feel these emotions. You can acknowledge them but you shouldn't give in to them or work on them. Just continue what you are doing and these emotions will pass.

3. Reduce distractions around you.

I have discussed earlier how your environment can affect your productivity. Your workplace can also help you avoid procrastination by reducing the distractions around you. Without your phone at your reach, the tendency of you answering text messages and attending to notifications and thus postponing your work is minimized. As I have said, we have a limited capacity to control our impulses so let us just control our environment instead.

4.   Focus on the reason why you are doing something.

Most of the time, knowing why you are doing something and for whom you are doing it is enough for you to get motivated to finish a project. So the best thing you can do is remind yourself of these reasons. When I was in college for instance, I placed pictures of other people graduating on my calendar to remind myself that whatever I am doing will lead me to my graduation. Now that I am older, I write books and go to work to provide a good life for my children. By reminding ourselves of what is in it for us and how a task can benefit us, we become less likely to procrastinate.

Procrastination may have become a habit for you but it is good to know that procrastination is a permanent sickness. When we procrastinate, we already know that a certain task is important; we just have to have the determination, the discipline and of course the decision to really start and finish it.

Chapter 7
Focusing on the Task at Hand

No other time in history are the human beings bombarded with so many distractions and disturbances than what we are experiencing today. We have television in our homes and radios in buses all waiting to be heard. We have computers in our desk carrying the new emails it wants to show you. Then there are smart phones that are constantly in our pockets if not in our hands, that has text messages waiting for a reply, calls waiting to be answered and endless notifications from all social media sites waiting t0 be acknowledged. With everything that is going on in our life, it is very easy to lose focus. Which is why to master the skill of time management, one needs to know how to fine-tune his/her focus on the task.

Concentration or focus on a certain tasks is one of the critical elements for success. Contrary to popular opinion, our brain's performance on tasks are diminished when it multi-tasks. Thus, you have to learn how to focus your attention to where it is needed and these are some tips to help you how.

1.   Work in a quiet place.

Today, there seems to be no quite place anymore. There is always that constant hum of computers, the rings of the telephone and the sounds from the television. These sounds can reduce your ability to concentrate, will keep you off what you are doing and can definitely diminish your performance. So my suggestion would be to find yourself the quietest place you can use. For instance, you can place your home office as far as possible from the entertainment room or play room where there is likely to be noises from the children. In the office, you can keep your door shut to minimize the noise when you are working on something critical. If you really can't do anything about some of the noise, what you can do is play white noise on the background to tune out the distracting ones.

2. Start your day early.

Do you know why we tend to be very productive when we wake up early? Aside from the fact that our energy levels are higher when we wake up together with the sun, there are also fewer distractions in the morning. There are less cars speeding in the highway, there are no phone calls, there are no text messages and the only sound you will ever hear is the chirping of the birds. The earlier you begin your day, the lesser the interruptions you encounter because I know that you can definitely confirm how the problems and challenges increases while the day progresses. So make it a habit to jumpstart your day early when there is still no rush-hour traffic, fewer people at their desks and no phones ringing. You cannot only save time by doing so but you can also start ahead of others.

3.   Have shorter but more frequent breaks.

Our concentration also has its limitation. We cannot work straight for very long hours and still produce optimum results. One important reason why I asked you to factor in flex time in your calendar is for you to gain you concentration back too. There are some jobs that can drain us eventually that we would need breaks every now and then. Don't worry about the time you waste when you take breaks because when you go back to your work, you will definitely feel more energized and have your focus returned. A word of caution though, never overdo your breaks as it can turn into procrastination.

4.   Practice dismissing distracting thoughts.

We cannot stop the thoughts that come into our mind because they just flow like water that come and go. Sometimes, while doing something, we might catch ourselves thinking about this weekend's plans or the new movie showing later in the evening. When these thoughts come, acknowledge them and then dismiss them. To do this, simply focus on your breathing and nothing else. Allow these thoughts to slip past your consciousness until you are holding onto your breathing only. Do this for a few minutes and I guarantee that this mindfulness training will help you find your focus again.

5. Control your personal interactions.

The founder of Ford, the US-based car manufacturing company, used to implement a "no-talking" rule among its workers to increase their productivity. So as these workers stand beside each other near the conveyor belt, they cannot open their mouths but just focus on what they are doing instead. This rule was believed to have started the art of ventriloquism or the making of sounds without the opening of the mouth. One important lesson we will learn here is that social interaction is a basic need and one way or another, we will always try to communicate with other people. This is a phenomenon we often see in the office with people pouring over the photocopy machines sharing the latest gossip when the boss is not around. Yes, these interactions can help us create and maintain friendships but this can also compromise our productivity. So what you can do is to control these personal interactions by not staying too long in the discussion and honestly telling your colleagues that you still have something to do. Another measure you can implement is the "Do Not Disturb" sign I have mentioned earlier so that your friends will not come knocking on your office while you are concentrating on your work.

6. Give yourself rewards for success.

Rewards have such an amazing effect on people. Do you know that it can drive performance more than punishment does? Knowing this fact, you should now start giving yourself rewards to encourage yourself to take on bigger goals. For instance, you can give yourself even a square of chocolate for every hour that you are productive. I'm sure there are some other things you want so transform these wants into motivators for you to do your tasks. When there are rewards waiting for you in the end, there is little possibility for you to lose your drive in finishing the task.

Time management is a skill in itself. Concentration is a skill in itself as well that is not only needed in time management but in other aspects of life too. So you better make sure to practice how to focus solely on the task you have at hand and you will reap your benefits – definitely.

Chapter 8
Starting Time-Efficient Practices

Actually, every guideline and tip I have mentioned in the previous chapters is intended for the efficient use of your time. They are all skills that you need to acquire. For instance, setting goals, prioritizing tasks, scheduling activities, maintaining your workplace, combating procrastination and mastering focus and concentration are all skills that you must have to truly master time management.

Although time management is about 70 percent skills, it is also 30 percent habit. Thus, in this chapter, we will be discussing some time efficient practices or habits that can contribute to the improvement of your time management skill. Here are seven of the most time efficient practices you can adopt. Some of these are familiar since they are already discussed in the previous chapter.

1.   Starting your day early.

As I have said in the previous chapter, starting your day early can help you be productive because there are little distractions early in the morning and you can take advantage of your high energy levels. You can start right now by adjusting the alarm on your phone or clock so that it will wake you up earlier. It will be hard for the first three days perhaps but your body clock will eventually adapt to the schedule. You will eventually realize that waking up before anyone else is really a habit that can increase your productivity.

2. Planning for the next day.

For every minute you spend planning, you save ten times in the execution. This definitely holds true in time management so you better take ten minutes of your day right before you go to sleep and plan the thing you have to do for the next day. Make sure to follow the guidelines in planning I have mentioned earlier including scheduling the most important activities during your prime time and including some flex time on the equation.

3. Taking care of your health.

When you work so hard to be productive and has compromised your health in the process, all the time you think you have saved have just gone to waste. If you get sick, you probably have to miss several days of work and have to move all the tasks in your calendar. Aside from costing you your time, getting sick can cost you more money. So don't try and work beyond what your body is capable of and don't forget to put meal times, rest periods and sleep in your calendar, as well.

4.   Learning to say no.

When you created the first draft of all the tasks you think you need to do in the earlier chapter, you probably discovered how there were items that aren't really important to you but you still find urgent. These tasks are most likely none of your business at all but are just tasks other people requested you to do. If that is the case, then you probably kept on saying yes to people. You continue this behavior and you will end up not doing the important things you need to do because you are too busy doing more things for others. For your own benefit, learn how to say no every now and then. Simply say that your plate is full and you cannot take any more tasks as of the moment. Remember to sound really sincere as well and they will surely understand.

5.   Delegating tasks.

If the tasks you have at hand are still too much for you, then you probably need to delegate some of them. Choose those tasks that are not so critical or those that you think that someone else can do better. Don't ever think that delegating tasks is a sign of weakness. Instead, see it as a sign of wisdom – the wisdom that sometimes you need to accept the fact that you are face with limitations and you have to give up some tasks to make room for the more important ones.

6.   Simplifying life.

Life is better when live simply, do you agree? Living a simple life will definitely help you when you want to practice time management in your life. A simple life comes with fewer possessions and fewer possessions translate to fewer distractions. Therefore, there will be less things vying for your attention for you to breeze through your day smoothly. What's more is that when you become contented living a simple life, you don't have to have too many tasks and responsibilities on your table.

7.   Starting fresh every day.

One important lesson you have to learn in time management is that you should not fail on your past failures and start each day anew. We may sometimes fail to meet our schedules for today or not be as productive as we hoped to be but we should not be discouraged and continue to still plan for tomorrow. Believe in your power to recover the time you have lost and trust that you can do better the next day.

When you are just diligent to practice these habits, they will eventually become routine for you making it easier each day.

Chapter 9
Avoiding Time-Wasting Habits

We already have tackled effective ways on how you can use your time wisely and be productive but you might still encounter problems with some of your old habits. What usually eat lots of our precious hours are useless habits. Some of these habits we do to kill time or procrastinate but some we do not even know existed and these are the most dangerous ones.

We must learn to identify what these time-wasting habits are so that we can avoid doing them again in the future. Here are the eight most common time-wasting habits that you should know better to avoid.

1.   Multitasking

Several studies suggest that more tasks we have on our hands at the same time, the poorer are outputs become. The theory here is that we humans have very limited attention resources and we do better when we attend to just one stimulus. Our limitation as human beings then makes multitasking a time-wasting habit for us. Not only do we perform poorly at our tasks, we also increase the likelihood of repeating the tasks we thought we have completed because they didn't meet our standards.

2. Working continuously for long periods

Again, we have limited attention resources so eventually our focus and concentration on a task eventually die out. I used to commit this mistake a lot of times before, just staring blankly at my computer screen for hours even when no matter how hard I try, I just can squeeze any new idea. I could have spent those hours relaxing my brain looking at the trees outside my window. The renewal of my concentration could just have taken minutes! Working nonstop can be a very bad habit for you especially when things like this happen. Try to avoid this bad habit by factoring in flex time in your calendar to renew your focus and maximize your productivity.

3. Obsession on perfection

An obsession on perfection can be very crippling and limiting. When we don't start a project just because we are not yet sure whether it will turn out as perfect, we are just giving ourselves a poor excuse to procrastinate. Being very obsessed on perfection can be such a waste of time when we can use our hours and minutes to start the project and even have room for modification. Remember that if a project is not perfect when we you have ample of time to make it, it will be eons from perfection when you are cramming it.

4. Worrying too much

Worrying is such a huge time waster that can affect our success and happiness in life. When we worry, we do nothing but just think about the things we couldn't control. We already know that we cannot control it so why do we spend so much time thinking about it? If we use the time we worry to prepare for the things we worry about, we could have been more productive.

5. Always hurrying and not thinking

We usually hurry because we do not want to waste any time but when we constantly rush ourselves without even thinking, we end up spending too much time during the execution. In other words, time constraints should not compromise our ability to think about the situation and prepare for our actions. Through planning ahead, we can eliminate problems even before we start and save time righting wrongs as well.

6.   TV shows and video watching

Let me ask you, how many hours on average do you spend watching movies every day? Or how many hours do you spend watching videos on YouTube in your time at work? These TV shows and videos can get so much of our time without us knowing and we could have done something productive.

7.   Surfing the web

Surfing the net is even worse that watching TV. At least in the TV, we know it is late when the news program starts but when we surf the internet, we become glued to the monitors until our eyelids drop. "Just a few more posts/tweets," we often say to ourselves but then the few we promise can turn into hundreds. Yes, the internet is very helpful but we have to monitor our usage else we suffer dire consequences when we end up wasting too much time.

8.   Dealing with negative people

Just as negative thoughts can pull you down, so are negative people. These people can pull your energy level down, can color your outlook, can decrease your enthusiasm and most of all, they can reduce your productivity. These type of people are poison to your well-being so you would be better off to cut your ties with them for a happier and more productive you.

Do you know why most people consider time management very hard? It's because they think that time is out of their control. But the skills and habits I have presented to you are proof that no other person is in control of the situation than you. Always remind yourself that you are the master of your time and you can use it to your benefit.

CONCLUSION

Thank you again for downloading this book!

With the numerous guidelines, tips and strategies I have presented above, time management may come out as a tedious skill to learn. It can really require your patience, diligence and consistency. However, you will only encounter these difficulties at the beginning and time management actually becomes easier over time. I hope you won't give up as proper time management today will translate to success in the future.

Finally, if you enjoyed this book, then I'd like to ask you for a favor, would you be kind enough to leave a review for this book on Amazon? It'd be greatly appreciated!

Click here to leave a review for this book on Amazon!

Thank you and good luck!